Angels

— and —

Devas

A Compilation from books by
Torkom Saraydarian

TSG Publishing Foundation, Inc.

Angels and Devas - A Compilation
© 2001 The Creative Trust

ISBN: 0-929874-86-2

Printed in the United States of America

Cover Design:	*Nurhan Thompson* Phoenix, Arizona
Printed by:	*Print Partner* Phoenix, Arizona
Published by:	T.S.G. Publishing Foundation, Inc. Post Office Box 7068 Cave Creek, Arizona 85327-7068 United States of America www.tsg-publishing.com

Note: Meditations, visualizations, and other health information are given as guidelines. They should be used with discretion and after receiving professional advice.

This compilation was reprinted by permission of the copyright owner from the following books:
- *The Ageless Wisdom*, pp. 115 157
- *Challenge for Discipleship*, pp. 61, 326, 464-465
- *The Flame of the Heart*, p. 206
- *Joy and Healing*, p. 108
- *New Dimensions in Healing*, pp. 6, 543-562, 563-566
- *Other Worlds*, p. 55
- *The Psyche and Psychism*, pp. 87, 725
- *Spring of Prosperity*, pp. 22, 62
- *Talks on Agni*, p. 102, 181-182, 252, 253
- *Thought and the Glory of Thinking*, p. 284

Angels and Devas

Psychic energy is ... transmitted by angels. They are powerful transmitters or even sources of psychic energy. When a person is charged with psychic energy, he turns into a source of creative, healing, and enlightening energy.

Life proceeds stage by stage, gradually building more complicated forms. Evolution proceeds in many lives. Not all evolutions are on one direct path. There is human evolution; there is deva evolution; there are other evolutions which eventually merge.

On the lowest stage of devic or angelic evolution are found elementals and nature spirits which start on the involutionary path and then enter the path of evolution. Thus elementals are on the involutionary arc, and with their substance they build our physical, emotional, and mental bodies.

By being used age after age in the physical, astral, and mental bodies, elementals gradually develop elemental consciousness, and their evolution starts. Ages later, these elementals graduate and individualize in the form of nature spirits — as brownies, then elves, gnomes, mannikins, undines, sea spirits, and finally fairies. After they reach the stage of fairies, they evolve into sylphs, then into devas or angels.

Angels or devas are divided into two sections: lesser and higher angels. Lesser angels operate on the lower mental plane. Higher angels operate on abstract levels of the mental plane. Sylphs operate in the astral plane. It is after angels graduate from the higher mental levels that the angelic and human evolutions become parallel, until they reach the stage of Chohans, the stage of the Sixth Initiation, where both evolutions merge.

Nature spirits live in the earth, in water, in the air, and in fire. They have only one element in their nature: they are earthy, watery, airy, or fiery. Nature spirits identify themselves with the earth, with flowers and trees, with lakes and rivers, with the clouds, or with fire. Sometimes they ensoul such forms. They are harmless, but they do not like to be controlled by man.

Nature spirits abhor the pollution of the earth, water, and air. Thousands of them leave the areas polluted by human ignorance. They hate to see the trees, bushes, and flowers cut. They hate to see radiation contaminate the earth. They hate to see chemicals in the waters of the earth. They have their own territories, and they think that human beings have no right to destroy Nature. When they leave a place, natural calamities hit that place.

Elementals and Man

Man has four elements in his nature: earth, water, air, and fire. If all these elements are in harmony and highly developed, man will attract four kinds of devas and he will be successful in all the fields of the four elements. But in general, one of the elements predominates, and man will have to deal with the field which the element presents. If man is "earthy," he will be helped by earth elementals to have wealth, money, etc. If the water element predominates, he will be helped by water elementals, and he will be more occupied with the emotional field. If the air element predominates, he will be helped by air elementals to increase his mental knowledge. If the fire element predominates, he will be helped by the fire elementals in creative works and spiritual virtues. Food, water, various emotions, thoughts, and virtues or vices increase or decrease the elements existing in our bodies.

It is also noticed that these elements change when we relate with people. People sap our elements or increase them.

Devas are higher than nature spirits, and they are found on different levels. There are devas who live in the lower mental sphere, those who live in the higher mental sphere, and those who live in the higher astral levels. We are told that their language is color and music. Those human souls who can tune to the lower mental plane, or who can ascend there either after they sleep or after they die, can enjoy the presence of such devas, especially their music and the combination of colors which they produce with their thoughts.

Higher devas, or those who live on the higher mental levels, are far advanced devas. People who can raise their consciousness to the higher mental spheres can be impressed by these shining souls.

Beyond the higher mental plane there are the angels who cooperate with the Masters of the Wisdom, and they often help Them with Their plans.

What Service Do Angels Do?

1. They provide food for human beings and for animals in the form of vegetables and fruits, if they want to help them.

2. They provide etheric, astral, and mental food:
    a. Etheric-physical food is prana, which they transmit from the Sun or from the earth to human beings.
    b. Emotional food is love, aspiration, compassion, fearlessness, daring, courage, etc.
    c. Mental food is inspirations, impressions, ideas, thoughts, new revelations.

3. They help certain people in extremely critical conditions, saving them from drowning, fire, earthquakes, and hurricanes.

4. They lead people into right paths. They lead armies if the armies are fighting for Beauty, Goodness, and Righteousness.

5. They inspire musicians with new melodies, songs, symphonies, etc. Some musicians are even able to hear the music of angels and record it.

6. They inspire artists, imparting new ideas and enabling them to see new colors.

7. They inspire scientists with new laws and discoveries through the means of the Intuition and impression.

8. They inspire in a person Beauty, Goodness, Righteousness, Joy, Freedom, purity, and solemnity. Actually, they can inspire all the virtues in him once the person shows his real merit.

9. They preside over countries, states, towns, villages, homes, families, churches, groups, and fraternities dedicated to the human cause.

10. They overshadow mountains, lakes, rivers, springs, oceans, and forests.

11. They heal people directly or indirectly. They even adjust their centers, glands, and nervous system and produce harmony and health.

12. They communicate in dreams and take the worthy one into subjective meetings, various sacred places, or higher Ashrams.

Some angels energize and charge the sacred places of worship and stay there for days and months to inspire and heal people. They charge Ashrams and enlighten people's minds; they emanate love energy to unite them as a living whole. They also protect Ashrams from dark attacks.

What Can Man Do for Angels?

Angels nourish themselves from elements which man provides. Man can help angels by providing them with the following nourishing elements:

1. Thoughts expressed in music, painting, poetry, writings, dances, singing, or meditation. They greatly enjoy the electrical emanations during individual or group meditation. Lofty thoughts are their primary food.

2. Joy, love, and the emanations of feeling free.

3. Any dedicated, sacrificial, heroic labor because in such a labor man emanates certain elements which nourish them.

Angels live under the law of righteousness and gratitude. Whatever they receive, they offer equal gifts to man in various forms.

What Do Angels Hate?

Angels hate the pollution of the earth, water, air, and Space. Any protection of the environment gives them extreme joy. They do not want people to destroy forests, flowers, or bushes because these are their own creative work which they offer to living forms for their survival and enjoyment. It is through forests, trees, bushes, and flowers that the energy and influence of the angels reach human beings, heal their wounds and impart to their hearts new visions of a better future.

Angels hate for the water to be polluted. Water elementals are the essence of the water. Pollution makes them withdraw, and the water loses its healing and refreshing essence. When water is polluted, it affects the soil, vegetation, and even the air.

Angels do not want wars, disunity, or cleavages between nations, between families, and within families. Any cleavage creates disturbances in the angelic worlds. Unity and harmony give them delight.

Angels hate the pollution of the air. They cannot easily help humanity if people are living in pollution. When devas withdraw from a certain location because of earth, water, and air pollution, crime increases there. People lose their source of guidance and inspiration and live an anti-evolutionary life. They fall into vices and slowly lose their sense of values and their sense of direction. They waste their time, energy, bodies, and money, and gladly face the path of degeneration and insanity.

Angels hate the pollution of Space. Through wrong and criminal thoughts, hatred, and bloodshed, people pollute the Space and prevent the currents of light, love, and direction from reaching them.

Angels do not like to be close to those people whose secretions are malodorous and poisonous. Such a condition occurs in people because of their conflicting emotions, guilt feelings, hatred, malice, slander, and treason. Purity of the aura attracts them.

Bedrooms that have various odors repel them. This is why Oriental Sages advise sleeping in the open air if one is not in danger of various pollutions. Sleeping in mountains, deserts, forests, or near the shores of lakes or rivers gives an opportunity to higher beings to come closer to you. Bedrooms must be simple and almost vacant, away from odors, decaying materials, and mechanical noises.

Angels are repelled by places where sewage flows or stagnant water, dead animals, blood, urine, or waste materials exist. They like well-ventilated rooms, where odors and different smells do not exist. They do not like the smell of meat or barbecues. They do not like the smell of burned food. They are also repelled by irritation, anger, and violent emotions. Once when I was angry and irritated, my grandmother said to me, "Do not disturb your invisible friends."

Great Chohans have armies of angels who help Them. These armies are totally oriented toward the service of the Plan, and they study the Divine Purpose. They also fight against the armies of dark forces. Such fights are recorded as "wars in heaven."

We are told that Christ has an enormous army formed of many grades of angels, and in critical times He mobilizes this army to protect humanity from the attacks of dark forces.

Angels are especially active at full moon times, especially at the time of the Aries, Taurus, and Gemini full moons. The highest moment of these three full moons is the Wesak Festival at which time the Angelic Hierarchy cooperates with the Spiritual Hierarchy. Thousands of these angels are dispatched to various places on earth to channel the energy of Wesak for the upliftment of humanity. A great Sage suggests that one must not allow himself to miss observing the Wesak Festival at the right moment of the Taurus full moon.[1]

Communication with Higher Worlds gradually becomes more difficult as the moral pollution accumulates. Like a fog around the earth, it hinders the communication between the two worlds and affects humanity in general to such a degree that eventually clearing this moral fog becomes impossible. This leads humanity toward suicide or total destruction.

the earth. Just as angels hate the pollution of the earth, water, air, and Space and withdraw further into Space, a similar thing happens in a person when he pollutes his physical body with alcohol, drugs, unhealthy sexual practices, etc.; when he pollutes his emotional body through hatred, fear, anger, greed, jealousy, revenge; and when he pollutes his mental body with vanity, prejudices, separatism, pride, and ego. In such conditions, the Inner Guardian withdraws and darkness descends on the path of the person.

Angels love calmness, serenity, gentleness, poise, solemnity, and grace. Whenever they see such qualities in someone, they are attracted to him and pass to him their joy, blessings, and protection.

Some people have angelic elements in their speech, actions, and expressions. Beyond what they are, they have something which cannot be put into words: they have an angelic element which is magnetic, graceful, inspiring, and strengthening. Some people are surrounded by a group of angels,

---

1. For information on full moons, refer to the *Symphony of the Zodiac.*

and the presence of such people brings joy, solemnity, understanding, gratitude, and ecstasy.

Angels affect people through their presence, even if they do not talk. Their invisible influence spreads like a fragrance. Psychic energy is also transmitted by angels. They are powerful transmitters or even sources of psychic energy. When a person is charged with psychic energy, he turns into a source of creative, healing, and enlightening energy.

Angels especially help those who teach the pure Teaching of the Hierarchy to increase Beauty, Goodness, Righteousness, Joy, and Freedom in the world. They stand beside such people and strengthen their aura with their angelic emanations. They protect them from dark attacks. They remind them of special events or points in their memory. They can even connect them to higher spheres for greater inspiration and ideas or for energy.

Sometimes a group of angels performs various duties. For example, during a lecture, some angels regenerate the memory. Some of them impart ideas. Some of them charge the words of the lecturer with their own energy. They purify the space over the audience. They insulate the mental lines of certain people who are connected with dark forces. Some of them impart joy, enthusiasm, and the spirit of unity. Thus they uplift the whole audience.

Certain angels serve as connecting links between the lecturer and his Master, or between the mind and the Intuitional Plane of the lecturer. On rare occasions, it is even experienced that they urge the Solar Angel of the lecturer to take control and speak through the lecturer himself instead of through his soul.

In extremely rare conditions, angels enter into the aura of a person and use him at certain critical times, after they get permission from the person's Solar Angel.

Angels sometimes even protect holy places or certain houses by standing guard at the door or windows and directing enemies to different paths. In certain cases, they provide money, food, paper, and books. They make you discover lost objects and find people whose addresses were unknown.

People have created ways and means to control angels and use them for their own personal ends. The real Teaching is against such actions. You must provide the right conditions for the angels to help, since they are there to help you.

Angels love the beauty of gardens, flowers, natural colors, music, and fragrance. Music is very important to them. They like to enjoy music or paintings that carry a spiritual charge from the artist. If the artwork is created from a high spiritual level and by a person who is charged with lofty ideas and visions, the music or painting carries a great power for them, a great nourishment and joy. They dwell in those areas where great music and art in various forms are created or performed.

Angels especially love the fragrance of rose, musk, freesias, violets, amber, and frankincense. They love the natural fragrance emanating from a person full of joy and ecstasy.

Devas and angels love fountains, waterfalls, rocks, and precious stones. They love beeswax candles, flames, and incense, especially sandalwood and rose. They love live flowers and little plants in your home, especially little pine trees. They love melodious music, paintings, statues built by great artists, and Oriental and Indian carpets.

Noise is very repelling to angels, especially the noise of machinery. They also hate the noise rising from a group or a crowd of people where everyone is talking with everyone else. In ancient times Teachers told us that when people gather together they are allowed to do the following things:

1. Keep silence

2. Meditate

3. Sing together

4. Listen to a lecture or music

5. Pray together in unison

Angels do not like applause. Applause shatters their vehicles and the sphere of electricity which they build over the audience if the audience is in ecstasy and united in the spirit of the lecture or other performance. Very soon applause will be outmoded when a certain number of persons realize the damage done by it.[2]

Angels abhor treason, gossip, malice, and slander. They especially do not forgive a person who denies the Hierarchy or speaks blasphemous words against Great Ones. In such cases, they leave the person to face his dark destiny alone.

Heavenly hosts are divided into nine major sections by some Church Fathers. They are called:

1. Seraphim

2. Cherubim

3. Thrones

4. Dominions

5. Virtues

6. Powers

2. See also "Art and the Subtle Worlds" in *Other Worlds.*

7. Principalities

8. Archangels

9. Angels

Each group has the field of its administration and its sphere of power and responsibility.

1. *Seraphim* are related to the energies of Cosmic Love and to Christ, and they are active in His Plan.

2. *Cherubim* are related to the Universal Mind, the Holy Spirit, and psychic powers.

3. *Thrones* are related to Cosmic Will, the Will of the Father.

4. *Dominions* are the supervisors of the economy of the solar system and agents of supply and demand.

5. *Virtues* are related to Cosmic Principles and laws.

6. *Powers* are related to the Law of Karma, and they try to transmute evil into good.

7. *Principalities* are protectors or supervisors of continents, races, nations, tribes, cities, towns, etc.

8. *Archangels* are representatives of the Seven Rays and the heads of the seven kingdoms in Nature. They are the spirit of sacred planets. The duty of archangels is to contemplate the Divine Purpose and work for its manifestation.

9. *Angels* are of various groups and of various duties.

The nine groups of angels, who are agents of Divine Law and transmitters of Divine Will, were once upon a time human beings, not necessarily on the physical plane, but maybe on finer globes and in the astral or mental planes. Through the human evolution they developed intelligence, and now they consciously serve the Divine Purpose and Plan.

Solar Angels are not the same as angels. Solar Angels were human beings in past manvantaras. They are on the line of human evolution and are very advanced Initiates. They are related to the Karmic Lords, to the Hierarchy, and to the intelligence aspect of the First, Second, and Third Rays.

No angel can relate to a human being before he gets permission from the person's Solar Angel, Who has complete information regarding the karma of the particular person.

Angels do not obsess or possess people, but they can inspire and help if for a certain reason the Solar Angel cannot reach the human soul. In general, angels have their own duties and responsibilities, and they do not interfere with human life except if an order is given to them to do so.

Not only can a person's Solar Angel leave him, but the human soul can even leave the personality. In this case, the personality lives like an automaton through recorded urges and drives, or it becomes the apparatus of a low-level entity which possesses it and uses it for its own advantage to experience sex, alcohol, various crimes, etc. before its own incarnation.

Some criminals and materialists continuously stay on this earth. They die, but the next moment they are born again through one who provides a proper channel for them. They constantly go through suffering and depravity until one day their karma allows them to pass to the Subtle World.

Angels in general protect the human family from the attacks of dark forces. When people fight against each other, angels feel sad but they do not interfere. But if dark forces attack human beings, angels protect them from the dark forces — if the attack is not generated by the karmic liabilities of the person.

If you are walking on the path of righteousness, angels indirectly help you to fight your own battles by illuminating your mind, strengthening your heart, and inspiring your soul.

The whole Angelic Hierarchy is fiery, and human beings are warned not to force a contact with them. If they want to appear for certain reasons, they prepare the person through certain vibrations and they slowly appear. When they appear, their message is related to global problems and international service. They are not interested in your petty problems.

We are told that certain dark entities take the form of angels and appear to those whose vanity they can use for certain purposes. Many false directions have been given by such entities throughout the ages, and many books are channeled by them to their servants. One must be extremely careful to recognize these wolves in sheepskins.

There are many signs by which you can recognize such imposters. Some of them praise you and feed your vanity. Some of them speak about your past lives. Some reveal the secrets of other people. Others advise you to take certain actions to satisfy your desires. Others tell you that you are a Messiah, a Christ, a prophet, to satisfy your desires. Still others try to dominate your will and give you orders. Others stimulate your sexual center or inspire hatred and revenge in your heart. Others create cleavages between you and the source of your vision. It is not strange that they have their followers among human beings who do the same things, following the examples of their bosses.

The dark angels work through their agents if they see that they cannot deceive you themselves. Sometimes it is easier to know them than to know their human agents, who have graduated from the "school" of the art of deception and who usually approach you as a friend, helper, etc.

Real angels are not involved in your personality problems. They are not interested in your past but in the Hierarchy, Shamballa, and the glorious Plan.

Just as there are angels who preside over families, cities, and nations, there are also dark ones who try to establish their own stations to hinder the labor of the real angels. Such dark ones can establish their headquarters in locations where there are whorehouses, gambling places, groups which are separative and criminal, nightclubs where alcohol is used, or places where drugs are used. Through the substance of people present in such places, dark ones come and anchor themselves in cities and towns, and from that date on, crime, sickness, and insanity increase there.

On the other hand, angels inspire Beauty, Goodness, Righteousness, Joy, Freedom, tolerance, gratitude, and striving. They strengthen their positions in a nation, city, or town when a certain amount of people dedicate their lives to the Common Good and the service of humanity. Thus there can be a close interrelation between angels and men if people transform their lives and work for the upliftment of humanity, for the cleaning of pollution, and for progressive achievements toward the Hierarchy of Light.

Free Will

Angels do not have free will. They form an army, and each member of the army obeys the Will of the Most High. Human beings have free will, but only in a certain sense:

when their will is fused with the Divine Will. Man must eventually resign from his free will, study the Will of the Most High, and live according to that Will. Christ achieved such a victory when He said, "Not my will but Thine be done." In that moment He fused His will with the Divine Will. From that point on, He had the most powerful energy under His control but also the pure wisdom to use it according to the direction of the Father.

Angels live in the stream of the Divine Will, and there is no conflict in them.

Humans think that without free will, no one can progress and advance, but they ignore the fact that freedom is not achieved except when one renounces his free will for the Divine Will. It is also true that if a totalitarian controls your will and you renounce your will, you will never advance on the path of evolution. Totalitarianism is not God's Will. The Will of God manifests as Beauty, Goodness, Righteousness, Joy, Freedom, solemnity, purity, and sincerity. Let these qualities control your will if you want to fuse with the Will of the Most High.

Do Angels Incarnate as Human Beings?

All spiritual beings existing beyond the present evolutionary state of human beings pass through human evolution. *The Secret Doctrine* states:

> ...In order to become a divine, fully conscious god, —
> aye, even the highest — the Spiritual primeval INTEL-
> LIGENCES must pass through the human stage. And when
> we say human, this does not apply merely to our terres-
> trial humanity, but to the mortals that inhabit any
> world, i.e., to those Intelligences that have reached the
> appropriate equilibrium between matter and spirit, as

we have now, since the middle point of the Fourth Root Race of the Fourth Round was passed. Each Entity must have won for itself the right of becoming divine, through self-experience....[3]

...The whole Kosmos is guided, controlled, and animated by almost endless series of Hierarchies of sentient Beings, each having a mission to perform, and who — whether we give to them one name or another, and call them Dhyan-Chohans or Angels — are "messengers" in the sense only that they are the agents of Karmic and Cosmic Laws. ...For each of these Beings either was, or prepares to become, a man, if not in the present, then in a past or a coming cycle (Manvantara). They are perfected, when not incipient, men; and differ morally from the terrestrial human beings on their higher (less material) spheres, only in that they are devoid of the feeling of personality and of the human emotional nature — two purely earthly characteristics. The former, or the "perfected," have become free from those feelings, because (a) they have no longer fleshly bodies — an ever-numbing weight on the Soul; and (b) the pure spiritual element being left untrammelled and more free, they are less influenced by maya than man can ever be, unless he is an adept who keeps his two personalities — the spiritual and the physical — entirely separated. The incipient monads, having never had terrestrial bodies yet, can have no sense of personality or EGO-ism....[4]

---

3. H.P Blavatsky, *The Secret Doctrine*, Vol. I (1978 ed), p. 106.

4. *Ibid.*, pp. 274-275.

"...Man can neither propitiate nor command the Devas," it is said. But, by paralyzing his lower personality, and arriving thereby at the full knowledge of the non-separateness of his higher SELF from the One absolute SELF, man can, even during his terrestrial life, become as "One of Us...."[5]

In sober truth, as just shown, every "Spirit" so-called is either a disembodied or a future man. As from the highest Archangel (Dhyan Chohan) down to the last conscious "Builder" (the inferior class of Spiritual Entities), all such are men, having lived aeons ago, in other Manvantaras, on this or other Spheres; so the inferior, semi-intelligent and non-intelligent Elementals — are all future men. That fact alone — that a Spirit is endowed with intelligence — is a proof to the Occultist that that Being must have been a man, and acquired his knowledge and intelligence throughout the human cycle. There is but one indivisible and absolute Omniscience and Intelligence in the Universe, and this thrills throughout every atom and infinitesimal point of the whole finite Kosmos, which hath no bounds, and which people call SPACE, considered independently of anything contained in it. But the first differentiation of its reflection in the manifested World is purely Spiritual, and the Beings generated in it are not endowed with a consciousness that has any relation to the one we conceive of. They can have no human consciousness or intelligence before they have acquired such, personally and individually....

The whole order of nature evinces a progressive march towards a higher life. There is design in the action of the seemingly blindest forces. The whole process of evo-

---

5. *Ibid.*, p. 276.

*lution with its endless adaptations is a proof of this.
The immutable laws that weed out the weak and feeble
species, to make room for the strong, and which ensure
the "survival of the fittest," though so cruel in their
immediate action — all are working toward the grand
end. The very fact that adaptations do occur, that the
fittest do survive in the struggle for existence, shows
that what is called "unconscious Nature" is in reality
an aggregate of forces manipulated by semi-intelligent
beings (Elementals) guided by High Planetary Spirits
(Dhyan Chohans), whose collective aggregate forms the
manifested verbum of the unmanifested* LOGOS, *and
constitutes at one and the same time the* MIND *of the
Universe and its immutable* LAW.[6]

It is generally understood that devas incarnate after a
certain stage of development on the mental plane. They can
carry on their evolution up to the Sixth Initiation, and there
they converge with human evolution. We are told that many
archangels became human beings and took the form of human
beings to evolve according to the archetype of the human
form.

It must be remembered that the invisible hosts in the
sphere of the earth are not only angels, devas, or spirits. There
are also various entities. There are those who were human
and are now living in various planes with their various bodies. There are those who were angels but incarnated as human beings and are now living in higher spheres as angelmen. There are those who are living around the earth but
are able to visit the subtle planes or appear to living human
beings. There are those who have graduated from human
evolution and are engaged in the work of the Hierarchical

6. *Ibid.,pp. 277-278.*

Plan. And, there are those who belong to the army of the dark forces.

All these entities are often called "angels," but they are not. One must have sharp spiritual vision to discriminate between them when one comes in contact with them.

Knowing these facts, one must not conclude that each experience with the invisible world is an experience with angels, though it is possible. There are many human souls working in the subtle planes as invisible helpers who are often mistaken for angels.

Archangels, with their own armies of angels, form subtle centers in Space to transmit certain energies to planets from higher sources. Archangels can also be visualized as rays, beams of light, currents of intelligent energy, the totality of which builds the network of communication between all existing forms and the Mysterious Beyond.

Archangels finished human evolution a long time ago. We are told that at present they are gaining experience with their bodies of manifestation which are the sacred planets.

In the Teaching of Great Ones, we read that some archangels failed on the path of their evolution. These failures must wait until a new solar system begins evolving and life there progresses to form human beings. It is at this stage that these great beings pay their karmic debts.

> ...Then they become an active Force, and commingle with the Elementals, or progressed entities of the pure animal kingdom, to develop little by little the full type of humanity. In this commingling they lose their high intelligence and spirituality of Devaship to regain them in the end of the seventh ring in the seventh round.[7]

---

7. *The Mahatma Letters*, A.T. Barker, ed., p.87.

It is stated in Plato's works that human beings can reincarnate as "animals." There is a great truth in this statement if it is understood rightly.

The great archangels entered human evolution and going beyond it became shining angels. It is easy to see what Plato meant in his statement.

We are told that the Buddhic and Atmic Permanent Atoms in the Spiritual Triad are connecting links between the human soul and two great angels. These angels share the human evolution and collect experiences and learning through these links. They also reflect the life of the human being as mirrors. Our Solar Angel is located mostly around the Mental Permanent Atom, thus forming the Spiritual Triad with the two great angels.

We can help these angels when we live a life of Beauty, Goodness, and Righteousness. One day we may form a part of this triangle, first locating ourselves at the center, then replacing our Solar Angel at the Fourth Initiation and becoming a part of this holy triangle, or the Spiritual Triad. When we reach this stage, our consciousness will have a greater chance to expand by assimilating the deep wisdom these great angels present to us.

The greatest lesson which man will teach these great angels is the principle of free will and the science of how to harmonize the free will with the Will of the Most High. These angels do not have free will, and they will learn about it by passing through the human kingdom. Through the study of the science of the will, man will realize the Oneness of life and the existence of the One Will and will consciously put it into action in all aspects of life.

Most human beings are not aware of such a cooperation between angels and men. We must remember that we are

always in the presence of three great angels, one human —
our Solar Angel — and two others from the angelic evolution. Even if in our daily struggles, successes, and failures we
do not feel their presence, they are there, in close contact
with our higher principles.

Until the Fourth Initiation, our Solar Angel becomes an
increasing source of inspiration. After the Fourth Initiation,
the human soul finds his greatest source of inspiration in
these great angels, and through them he reaches heights never
before imagined. They are the Divine Companions of man,
until he achieves Monadic consciousness. Greater glories are
waiting for him after that great achievement.

These great angelic beings do not have self-conscious-
ness or consciousness of individuality. They cannot understand why man centers all his activities around his individual
self-interests. Those who are selfish and who live their lives
centered in themselves will find it very hard to cooperate
and be inspired by these angels.

On the other hand, man must teach the angels the existence of and the secrets of the Self, not opposed to the One
Self but in harmony with the One Self. It is in this stage that
the angels will understand the mysteries of the *will*, the Self,
and freedom. Freedom is the ability to be one with the Cosmic Self.

Through purifying his being, man will be ready to learn
the selflessness of the angel. This can be understood only
when man passes through many lives under his false selves
and their interests, and eventually raises his pure Self into
the light of angelic selflessness.

Individuality is the goal of evolution. Each individual
instrument must achieve the purity of its sound to form part
of the Divine Orchestra and create the One Symphony.

Meditation and Angels

Meditation is a very safe way to attract the attention of angels. Meditation spreads peace in the body, emotions, and mind, harmonizes them, increases their vitality, and makes them more magnetic. Meditation raises the level of consciousness and makes it more sensitive to higher angelic impressions.

During meditation higher thoughts, ideas, and visions are attracted to the aura of the person. Such currents of higher thoughts create beautiful colors and radiations in the aura and send a signal of invitation to angels. As meditation deepens and the human consciousness enters into contemplation, the bridge between the two shores becomes shorter, and eventually the person finds himself in a blissful precipitation of higher currents of energies and ideas. This is how conscious contact between men and angels is established and how both can help each other's evolution.

Man must not try to bring invisible beings or angels to the sphere of the earth, but he must try to raise his own consciousness and meet them in their spheres.

Your intention in meditation must not be to force the angelic beings to come in contact with you. Such an intention in itself repels them. You must raise your consciousness, and things will happen naturally.

During meditation, you must be very careful to be focused in the higher mental plane, working with the pure substances of logic, reasoning, and intuitive perception. If you fall into the astral plane with a desire to meet angels, you will meet them; however, they will not be the ones you want to meet but rather those who will mislead you on your path.

Any extrasensory experience must be recorded clearly as it happened. Later, during the same day, you must study it and see whether it is a glamor, illusion, or attack. No experience must be taken as a signal of communication with Higher Worlds unless it proves to be so. The development and unfoldment of discrimination begins when the person faces subtle problems and tries to make a right judgement and take a right action.

Whenever you think that you are falling into glamor and are attacked by invisible forces, stop your meditation for a while and seek the advice of a Teacher.

You must also develop sensitivity to feel the presence of angels. It is not necessary to see them or hear them or touch them. You must first of all accustom yourself to feeling their presence. There are a few signs which are possible proofs of their presence:

1. Silence within yourself
2. A feeling of joy
3. A feeling of expansion
4. A feeling of oneness with all
5. A feeling of deep gratitude
6. A feeling of forgiveness
7. A sense of peace
8. A flow of creative ideas
9. Deeper contacts with sources of great ideas
10. Feelings of courage, daring, and striving
11. A feeling of self-renunciation
12. A feeling of being protected

These are some of the signs which indicate that angels are around you. When they depart, you feel depressed, abandoned, left alone in your destiny. You may feel dry, selfish, argumentative, egocentric, etc. Their presence gives you a feeling of blessing, inner abundance, and inner contentment.

You need not see them. You do not see electrical currents, certain radiations, perfumes — but you feel them. Often people see their own thoughtforms and imagination or the forms they desire. In reality, angels do not have a set form. They are currents of conscious energy, like beams or spheres of light. People cannot think about angels without creating an imaginative form for them. Thus they deceive themselves. It is time to annihilate a glamor which has dominated the human mind since the dawn of human civilization — the glamor which assumes that angels have human forms. They do not.

People say, "They don't have human forms, but they are dwarfs, silly looking elves, good looking fairies, etc." There is no truth behind these pictures. Such pictures are fabrications of those who never had an experience with angels.

Angels must not be confused with great, living Adepts or Masters, Who sometimes appear with Their glorious bodies around Their etheric or physical forms and Who often terrify the one who meets Them. They are sometimes higher than many angels, and They have deeper access to the Plan and the Purpose of the Most High. They not only have free will but also pure intelligence. Some of Them have many angels in Their Ashrams whom They teach.

Christ is called, "The Teacher of angels and men."

Angels enjoy learning and feeling high vibrations and emanations. That is why many of them attend lectures and visit halls where great music or singing is performed. They enjoy galleries of great art.

Certain angels love ceremonies and rituals because of the harmony and rhythm of color, sound, and movement. They not only like the ceremonies and rituals, but they also transmit energy to the celebrant, who distributes it to the audience. They even partake in ceremonies and rituals. They deeply love ceremonies of initiation when the neophyte repeats an oath and makes promises for a noble life. They serve and help those who are conducting the ceremonies and rituals and impart certain blessings and energy to each of the celebrant's actions.

Angels love to help lecturers by not only bringing them higher ideas but also by charging their voice and expressions with a magnetic energy.

Certain angels are called "comforters." Others are guides in the Subtle World for those who pass away and need guidance to familiarize themselves with the conditions of the Subtle World. Comforters work on both sides — with those who lost someone and with those who left behind their beloved ones.

How to Ask for the Help of Angels

The first requisite for help is a pure, sincere heart. As long as there are hypocrisy, self-interest, thoughts of exploitation, lies, and deception in your heart, angels are repelled by you.

First of all, we must know that angels see us as we are. We cannot ask for their help if we are trying to hide our motives or if we want to continue to live the way we were living in the past. We often need their help because we face difficulties which were the result of causes we put into action. We must not continue to create the same causes if we expect their help. This is why a self-confession is necessary before we ask for their help.

The second requisite for their help is not to have doubt in your mind — doubt about their existence or doubt that you are doing wrong by praying to them instead of praying to God. Remember that often you ask for the help of your friends, and you do not think you are doing wrong. You ask for the assistance of the police and other governmental officials instead of going to the President. The Angelic Hierarchy is designated to help people, like all the officials of the government. There is nothing wrong in going to an official whose duty it is to meet your special needs.

Angels like to communicate with you and help you if you create the right approach. But the amount of help they can give you is conditioned by your karma, by your ability to recognize the mistakes you made in the past, and by the attitude you hold in the present. If you are able to face yourself clearly and decide to walk the path of Beauty, Goodness, Righteousness, Joy, and Freedom, you can minimize the effect of your past karma and open the door of possibility wider to receive greater help from the angelic kingdom.

A similar prerequisite applies to other kinds of help. For example, you may need light and wisdom to solve certain problems. Or you may need deeper inspirations to create great artworks or to invent things that will help humanity. In all such needs for angelic help, you have to purify your motives, detach yourself from past failures, and decide not to follow the path which leads you toward self-defeat. When your motive is really pure, it shines like a magnetic light and attracts help.

You must also remember that if your needs are not answered, it does not mean that angels have rejected you. They cannot act against your karma, but they can help you to be strong and to understand the real issues. Also, for example, in having a disease it is well to remember that not all diseases are the result of your own karma; they may be the result of the karma of the world, whose debt you may be helping to pay.

Not all the difficulties and sicknesses on your path are the result of your mistakes. They can also be the result of your love, labor, and dedication carried out beyond the capacity of your bodies. There are also cases in which a person pays for the karma of others, in order to save a group or a nation. But in all these cases, angels can help you in various ways. The important thing is not really healing or solving problems or making discoveries; the important thing is the process of perfection and unfoldment that you go through during your sickness, problems, and difficulties because through them you gain the resources of your knowledge of light, not otherwise available.

How to Invoke Angels

1. Sit in a quiet place in your home or in Nature — under pine trees, near big rocks or waterfalls, or near a small fire.

2. Relax your body.

3. Take five deep breaths.

4. Keep mental silence for a few minutes.

5. Say *The Great Invocation* and three OMs.

6. Say with deep concentration and feeling:

O shining brothers of Light,
O magnetic servers of Love,
O carriers of the mighty Will of the Most High,
here I present my heart to you
with the fire of my aspiration,
with the fire of my sincerity.
I call upon your help.

May your light enlighten me.
May your love heal me.
May the energy of the will you carry
create integrity, harmony, and wholeness
in all my being.

May I share your peace.
May I share your joy.
May I share your beauty.
May I share your freedom.

O shining brothers of Light,
if it is the Will of the Most High,
in the name of Christ
let my body be healed.

Let my mind find the solution to problems.
Let my soul register the impressions of knowledge
you want to pass to me.
Let your energy flow into me,
O shining brothers of Light.

I will use your light,
your love,
your energy imparted to me
for the benefit of all humanity,
for the manifestation
of the Plan of Light and Love,
for the fulfillment of the Divine Will.

7. Sit in silence. Visualize their light surrounding you. You may register a special vibration, experience a healing or expansion of consciousness, or receive new ideas and visions.

8. After five minutes of silent contemplation, express your gratitude to the angels, saying:

    I offer my gratitude to you
    as a fragrance
    rising from the altar of my heart.

    May your blessed service expand
    all over the world.

    May a chance be given to me
    to cooperate with your labor.
    Gratitude and love to you.

9. Sound seven OMs

   In the following hours or days, you must record any new idea, visions, or healing given to you, directly or indirectly. The most important thing you must have is faith. Faith is the intuitive awareness that your voice reached them.[8]

It was said in antiquity, "All people are angels." Verily, people are the messengers of the far-off worlds. Hence great is their responsibility. They rarely take the responsibility of carrying that which is entrusted to them and are not even distressed at losing the treasure. Only a few individuals may sorrow that they have forgotten something they have heard. Let people not forget that they are messengers and a bond with the distant worlds. Such a consciousness in itself beautifies everyday life.[9]

An angel means a messenger in Space, a messenger from one star to another star, from one planet to another planet, or from one plane of existence to another plane of existence. You must fix in your mind that you came to this Earth with certain responsibilities. You have special responsibilities, and when you go to another planet you will have other responsibilities there. Do not think that when you leave your body, everything is ended.[10]

A pure thought ever ascends.

At the feet of Christ it blossoms, radiant....[11]

When you look at a blooming flower and feel great gratitude, imagine that you are in the presence of Christ. You will help to form His garden, which is composed of pure

8. *New Dimensions in Healing,* pp. 543-562.

9. Agni Yoga Society, *Brotherhood,* para. 278.

10. *Talks on Agni, Vol. I,* p. 252.

11. Agni Yoga Society, *Leaves of Morya's Garden,* Vol. I, para. 21.

thoughts. A Great One says that pure thoughts create flower formations and that a thousand devas come and dance around them.[12]

In esoteric literature, flowers have a double meaning. They stand for the actual flowers we have in our gardens. We should plant and care for these flowers because they help to beautify and purify our atmosphere. The devas love them and like to be near them. Flowers on the path also stand for blooming people....[13]

You are not this nose, this hair, this body, this ear. You are an angel, and because you are an angel you have a mission beyond the earthly troubles and disturbances....[14]

...Some voices attract Angels; others, evil spirits.[15]

We are told that joy is the food of Angels....[16]

Joy draws the attention of angelic hosts and the Great Ones. The emanations of joy enable the Invisible Ones to approach your sphere and directly communicate with you, inspire you, and help you. Your joy convinces Them that you will not misuse Their treasures; you will not bury the "talents," but make good use of them.[17]

---

12. *Talks on Agni, Vol. I,* p. 102.
13. *Ibid.,* pp. 181-182.
14. *Ibid.,* p. 253.
15. *The Ageless Wisdom,* p. 157.
16. *Ibid.,* p. 115.
17. *Joy and Healing,* p. 108.

In the mental plane you can find mental flowers and birds. It is very interesting that animals are not found there. Flowers are the works of devas. Devas create a thousand times more beautiful flowers and more colorful birds than what we see on earth. Such birds are often devas in bird-form.[18]

...The path of the flaming heart is sometimes a lonely path — lonely for the world, perhaps — but you are with God so you are not really lonely. Angels and Great Ones are always in your company.[19]

Devas help in various ways when you nourish them with your pure essence, with your pure emanations. For example:

1. They fill your sphere with great magnetism.

2. They link your mind with higher clouds of knowledge and information.

3. They remind you of things from the past which can be used in your creative speech.

4. They carry messages from your friends and from their Souls.

5. They warn you of dangers.

6. They open opportunities for you.

7. They protect your aura from the thoughts of your enemies.

Aspirants, disciples, and initiates will cooperate more and more with devas when their lives reach great levels of purification. The devas will directly teach us; they will become links between us and greater centers. In rare cases, they

---

18. *Other Worlds*, p. 55.
19. *The Flame of the Heart*, p. 206.

will even supply those articles which we need — a book, money, or other needed materials.[20]

Healing and Invisible Beings

Actually some of the angels will teach in the great centers of advanced study, and a section of them will directly teach the healing arts through sound, color, and motion.

People have forgotten that there are invisible hosts who work in hospitals, in private homes, and in Space to heal people, not only physically but also emotionally and mentally, and to bring peace and health in individual and social life. These invisible beings are called angels or devas, a section of which directly works with all those who have dedicated their lives to healing. These angels or devas heal in various ways:

1. They impress doctors and surgeons to take the right actions and impress their minds with the further steps needed in a particular situation.

2. They reveal new formulas and help researchers make new discoveries.

3. They vitalize the auras of the sick.

4. They advise the patient in dreams to take certain steps, to use certain herbs or methods to heal himself.

5. They reveal the cause of diseases through telepathic communication or direct revelation.

6. They activate certain elementals in the body to heal the person.

---

20. *New Dimensions in Healing,* p. 64.

7. They charge water, food, or certain objects which transmit their energies to the patient.

8. They heal through creating invisible colors and inaudible sounds around the patient.

9. They heal people through charging them with certain fragrances.

10. They transmit a great amount of psychic energy through inspiration or direct action on the centers.

11. They energize the life thread, the sutratma.

12. They protect the person from various attacks which are often directed to the sutratma and to the etheric centers.

13. They purify and heal the person through fusion. This fusion is on three planes:
   — etheric fusion
   — heart fusion
   — thought fusion
   Fusion brings a great amount of energy from the angels or devas into the personality vehicles and creates purification, harmony, and energy in them.

14. Angels help us to see the cause of our suffering and eliminate that cause, if the cause originates in our thoughts, emotions, or actions. Sometimes an illness brings us greater blessings.

15. Angels help patients through charging their doctor's aura. Many highly dedicated doctors immediately receive such charges when they come closer to the patient. Sometimes angels fuse their aura with the doctor's and charge his whole aura with healing energy.

16. Angels heal through music, inspiring certain composers to create music which at that particular time will prevent an epidemic, a cataclysm, or a war. Through such music, they purify and balance the fires of Space and bring safety to people.

We must remember that at this stage of our evolution angels do not work to make us physically immortal. Immortality will be achieved through human striving and efforts and evolution. But they try to help us learn our lessons, serve, and meet our responsibilities until the time when we must leave our bodies.

Our death is not a problem for the devas. We do not vanish from them when we leave our body. They obey the karmic laws, and they work in harmony for our evolution.

We are told that Great Ones have hundreds of angels under Their command through which They serve on greater and various fields.

The fear of death shocks them. They do not understand why we are so afraid of death. Our fears hurt them. Our anger and irritation cause repulsion in them. They understand our pain and suffering and try to help us.

Sometimes the angels do not heal us if pain and suffering are needed for our transformation and for an understanding of the deeper facts of life. But they help us to bear the suffering, learn great lessons, and obtain wisdom through the suffering. Their inspiration and presence make us courageous and help us face our problems with serenity, understanding, and even with joy.

People are sometimes surprised that their trouble evaporates immediately after the doctor visits them. Respect for doctors and faith in them facilitates the fusion of angelic auras with the aura of the doctors.

One of the great healing agents is the Mother of the World, the Blessed Virgin Mary, Who throughout centuries spread healing powers in every country, to every race.

There are also angels who protect travelers on horseback, on ships, in cars, or in airplanes. People are not aware that it was because of the help of an angel that their airplane landed safely, their car escaped a fatal accident, their horse did not fall into the abyss.... We have many reasons to be grateful for help never realized by us.

The help of the angels and devas cannot be listed completely because they have ways and means about which we have no idea; they work silently and without recognition. Our gratitude and faith in them are the only factors which give them joy.

Favorable conditions are needed for their effective work. For example:

1. Prayer and worship.
2. Inspirational reading.
3. Ceremonies and rituals. These attract them, especially if they are conducted in solemnity and with the beauty of sound, color, rhythmic movement, and pure thought.
4. Intense aspiration.
5. The fragrances of pine, frankincense, rose, freesias. These create a good atmosphere for their activities.
6. Meditation and group chanting. These are very conducive means for devic help.
7. Faith.
8. Joy, contentment, and the spirit of gratitude.

9. Water and fire. These are very conducive to their energies.

10. Certain stones such as the diamond, topaz, lapis, silver. These are magnetic to devic energies.

11. Fresh mountain air, forest air, the air near waterfalls are also very conducive of their energies.

12. Cleanliness of surroundings and clothing, live flowers, and small pine trees are a great help.

13. Relaxation of the mind, emotions, and body as well as silence are a great help.

14. A harmless spirit. This attracts the help of the angels.

15. One of the most effective factors is a strong decision to transform one's life. When the decision is real, it immediately attracts the healing angels who love purity, beauty, honesty, nobility, and righteousness. Changing one's heart toward Beauty, Goodness, Righteousness, Joy, and Freedom invites the angels immediately.

16. One of the greatest magnets for the healing energy of angels is a pure conscience or a pure heart which is not agitated by the memories of wrongs done to others or by wrong and harmful intentions for the future.

17. Love and compassion are strong magnets to attract angelic help.

18. Visitation to holy places, cathedrals, sacred mountains, and sacred rivers is a very effective way to come in contact with angelic presences.

19. Visitation to Holy Ones is another way to come in contact with angelic forces.

20. Certain books are directly connected with the angelic network, and reading and respecting them increases the possibility of contact with angels. Blessed objects and symbols are also very beneficial. Every blessing is a ray between the angelic hosts and the object.

In coming centuries the existence of angels will be experienced by millions of people. Actually, some of the angels will teach in the great centers of advanced study, and a section of them will directly teach the healing arts through sound, color, and motion.[21]

In an Oriental tradition, we are told that everyone has two angels; one sits on the right shoulder and the other one on the left shoulder. One is white, and the other is grey. The white one presents the path toward spiritual glory. The other one presents the path of moral and spiritual destruction. A person must discriminate between these two and choose the right angel, in order to follow the path leading to spiritual unfoldment.

Thus people always obey. The important thing is to know to whom or to what you offer your obedience.

One must obey the white angel for years or lives before the white angel gives him the freedom to obey the splendor of his own Inner Core.[22]

...Purified space is a very magnetic field, which attracts advanced angels and devas and radiates their blessings and joy, thus helping the process of healing and transformation.

---

21. *New DImensions in Healing*, pp.563-566.
22. *Challenge for Discipleshhip*, p.326.

The moment of confession and forgiveness creates an atmosphere into which are drawn various angels and dark forces. They wait anxiously to see what is going on. If the confessor is revealing the totality of himself with the right motive, with trust, and with regret about his own errors, the angels will rejoice; and they will inspire courage and reveal to him things related to Infinity and not related to short-range interests. But if the confessor, with various motives, wants to use the situation for his personality advantage, hiding the facts and his intentions, the dark forces will rejoice and inspire him to continue his treacherous path.

The moment of confession and forgiveness is a sacred moment, and one can be spiritually born again in such moments.[23]

The disciple must do regular meditation. Meditation is accumulative. Through meditation, you create a sphere of magnetic light around your head and around the place where you are sitting for meditation. This magnetic sphere attracts higher inspiration and devas who bring spiritual impressions to you from greater centers. The sphere of energy in the room attracts benevolent devas and this sphere turns into a source of energy, peace, and inspiration.

If you do not keep your meditation regular, this sphere of light around your head and in the room dissipates and vanishes. Then you must build it again when you restart your regular meditation. Also, Higher Beings may lose interest in you because of your instability and lack of persistence.[24]

---

23. *Ibid*, pp. 464-465.
24. *Ibid.,* p. 61.

When the heart is purified, the angels will receive you in the Subtle World and decorate your path with flowers and music.[25]

...Master Djwhal Khul says that devas can be contacted safely only on the Intuitional Plane. At the present, contact with the deva kingdom is becoming fashionable. This may have very destructive psychic consequences, since in order to safely make contact, one needs to work on the Intuitional Plane, rather than on the etheric or astral planes.[26]

...certain devas are related to us, and they can bring great inspirations and beauty to us if we are able to synchronize with them. The confusion, disorders or disturbances of our vehicles terribly upset them and they draw away from us. Our inharmonious vibrations repel them.

But if our vehicles radiate harmony of sound and color and rhythmic scintillations, they draw toward us and help us with their pure inspirations, energy, and healing powers.

Some devas receive their nourishment from human thoughts, emotions, and etheric emanations. If we are not healthy and do not provide pure and high quality food for them, we poison them or create heavy repulsion in them and thus deprive ourselves of their creative company.

We are told that certain devas come to the light and bring their beneficial influences to the bearer of light and to the location. They also love the radiation of fragrance because a natural fragrance emanates a symphony of colors which, when joined with prayers and lofty thoughts, creates a magnetic sphere in the room.[27]

---

25. Thought and the Glory of Thinking, p. 284.

26. *The Psyche and Psychism,* p. 87.

27. *The Psyche and Psychism,* p. 725.

...many fiery devas or angels ... work in close association with those whose lives are dedicated to Beauty, Goodness, and Truth. Through currents of impression and thought they bestow their help to such individuals.[28]

Harmlessness is a great treasure. As we increase our harmlessness, our aura shines with a splendid color. Devas love pure colors, and they give their inspiration and energy to you because of your pure color and fragrant emanation.[29]

---

28 *Spring of Prosperity,* p. 22.
29. *Ibid,* p. 62.

About the Author

Torkom Saraydarian (1917 – 1997) was born in Asia Minor. Since childhood he was trained in the Teachings of the Ageless Wisdom.

He visited monasteries, ancient temples, and mystery schools in order to find the answers to his questions about the mystery of man and the Universe.

He lived with Sufis, dervishes, Christian mystics, and masters of temple music and dance. His musical training included the violin, piano, oud, cello, and guitar. It took long years of discipline and sacrifice to absorb the Ageless Wisdom from its true sources. Meditation became a part of his daily life, and service a natural expression of his soul.

Torkom Saraydarian dedicated his entire life to the service of his fellow man. His writings and lectures and music show his total devotion to the higher principles, values, and laws that are present in all world religions and philosophies. These works represent a synthesis of the best and most beautiful in the sacred culture of the world. His works enrich the foundational thinking on which man can construct his Future.

Torkom Saraydarian wrote a large number of books, many of which have been published. All of his books will continue to be published and distributed. A few have been translated into Armenian, German, Italian, Spanish, Portuguese, Greek, Dutch, and Danish.

He left a rich legacy of writings and musical compositions for all of humanity to enjoy and benefit from for many years to come.

Visit our web site at www.tsgfoundation.org for interviews and additional information on Torkom Saraydarian.

Other Books by Torkom Saraydarian

- The Ageless Wisdom
- The Aura
- Battling Dark Forces
- The Bhagavad Gita
- Breakthrough to Higher Psychism
- Buddha Sutra — A Dialogue with the Glorious One
- Challenge for Discipleship
- Christ, The Avatar of Sacrificial Love
- A Commentary on Psychic Energy
- Cosmic Shocks
- Cosmos in Man
- The Creative Fire
- The Creative Sound
- Dialogue with Christ (2nd ed.)
- Dynamics of Success
- Dynamics of the Soul
- Education as Transformation, Vol. I
- Education as Transformation, Vol. II
- The Eyes of Hierarchy—How the Masters Watch and Help Us
- Flame of Beauty, Culture, Love, Joy
- The Flame of the Heart
- From My Heart — Volume I (Poetry)
- Glossary, A Concordance of Torkom Saraydarian's Works
- Hiawatha and the Great Peace
- The Hidden Glory of the Inner Man
- I Was
- Joy and Healing
- Karma and Reincarnation
- Leadership Vol. I
- Leadership Vol. II
- Leadership Vol. III
- Leadership Vol. IV
- Leadership Vol. V
- Legend of Shamballa
- The Mystery of Self-Image
- The Mysteries of Willpower
- New Dimensions in Healing
- Obsession and Possession
- Olympus World Report… The Year 3000
- One Hundred Names of God
- Other Worlds
- The Psyche and Psychism
- The Psychology of Cooperation and Group Consciousness
- The Purpose of Life
- The Science of Becoming Oneself
- The Science of Meditation
- The Sense of Responsibility in Society
- Sex, Family, and the Woman in Society, 2nd ed.
- The Solar Angel
- Spiritual Regeneration
- Spring of Prosperity
- The Subconscious Mind and the Chalice
- Symphony of the Zodiac
- Talks on Agni
- Talks on Agni, Vol. 2
- Talks on Agni, Vol. 3
- Thought & the Glory of Thinking
- Transformation
- Triangles of Fire
- Unusual Court
- Woman, Torch of the Future
- The Year 2000 & After

For all of Torkom Saraydarian's latest books and creative works visit our website at www.tsgfoundation.org

Booklets

- The Art of Visualization — Simply Presented
- The Chalice in Agni Yoga Literature
- Cornerstones of Health
- A Daily Discipline of Worship
- Discipleship in Action
- Daily Spiritual Striving
- Earrings for Business People
- Earthquakes and Disasters — What the Ageless Wisdom Tells Us
- Fiery Carriage and Drugs
- Hierarchy and the Plan
- How to Find Your Level of Meditation
- Inner Blooming
- Irritation — The Destructive Fire
- Mental Exercises
- Nachiketas
- New Beginnings
- Practical Spirituality
- Prayers, Mantrams and Invocations (now includes *Five Great Mantrams of the New Age*)
- Questioning Traveler and Karma
- Saint Sergius
- Synthesis

Booklets
(Excerpts and Compilations)

- Angels and Devas
- Courage
- First Steps Toward Freedom
- Prayers, Mantrams, and Invocations

Family Series Booklets

- Duties of Grandparents
- Cooperation
- Family Relations
- For Men
- For Women
- Ideal Marriage
- Responsibility
- Responsibilities of Fathers
- Responsibilities of Mothers
- Success
- The Heart of Your Partner
- Women as Torchbearers

Video and Audio Lectures

- The Seven Rays Interpreted
- Why Drugs Are Dangerous
- Complete list of lecture video and audio tapes by author available at **www.tsgfoundation.org**

Music

- A Touch of Heart (CD only)
- Dance of the Zodiac
- Far Horizons
- Fire Blossom
- Infinity
- Lao Tse
- Light Years Ahead
- Lily in Tibet
- Misty Mountain
- Piano Composition
- Rainbow
- Spirit of My Heart
- Sun Rhythms
- Tears of My Joy
- Toward Freedom
- 1994 Annual Convention Special Edition — Synthesizer Music

About the Publisher

T.S.G. Publishing Foundation, Inc. is a non-profit, tax exempt organization. Founded on November 30, 1987 in Los Angles, California, it relocated to Cave Creek, Arizona on January 1, 1994.

Our purpose is to be a pathway for self-transformation. We are fully devoted to publishing, teaching, and distributing the creative works of Torkom Saraydarian.

Our bookstore in Cave Creek and our online bookstore at our web site www.tsgfoundation.org offers the complete collection of the creative works of Torkom Saraydarian for sale and distribution.

Our newsletter *Outreach* contains thought-provoking articles and is available both in print and from our website with free email notification.

We also conduct weekly classes, special training seminars, and home study meditation courses.

Torkom Saraydarian Book Publishing Fund

Torkom Saraydarian dedicated his entire life to serving others in their spiritual growth. At the time of his passing, more than 100 manuscripts had been written and prepared for publication. This work represents a seamless tapestry of Wisdom and we are dedicated to publishing the entire collection.

He had the unique wisdom and dedication to write all of these magnificent books in one lifetime. Now it is our turn to do the work. Together we can make his dream a reality and bring his legacy to fruition.

We depend on contributions for the publishing of the books. A special fund, *The Torkom Saraydarian Book Publishing Fund* has been established for the completion of this legacy. Contact us for details about the *Book Fund* and an update regarding remaining manuscripts.

As we go to press with this book we have at least 75 titles not yet published! We need your help to release these treasuries of Wisdom.

You can contribute funds for an entire book, or give any amount you wish on a continuous basis or a one-time contribution.

Thank you for your loving and continuous support.

The Torkom Saraydarian University

Torkom Saraydarian dreamed of a training center, often calling it the **University**, where men and women can be trained in the theory and application of Higher Principles and Values of the Ageless Wisdom. He called such higher education "Aquarian Education" and continuously encouraged his students to form such an institution in the future.

There is an increasing need for leadership in the field of esoteric knowledge. More and more people are becoming disillusioned with the teachings given to them by opportunists, by people who have good intentions but are full of glamors and vanities, or by people who want to use the Teaching as a business to raise money.

Great damage is done to people who approach the Teaching with sincerity in their heart and are caught in groups, institutions, or organizations that are only for social activities or that function as traps for exploitation. Some of these searchers gradually forget about their quest and adapt themselves to their environment. Some of them totally suppress their aspiration and spiritual striving because of their disillusionment. Only a small percentage, through discrimination, continue their search to find the proper field where they can grow and serve.

The number of true searchers is increasing. We must prepare ourselves to meet their need and at the same time safeguard ourselves from the dangers of falling into vanities, glamors, or of using the searchers for our own interests.

Torkom Saraydarian, *Leadership I*, p. 16.

Our first training courses were launched in September 2000. We have classes on site as well as by correspondence. For information on classes and online registration visit our website at <u>www.TorkomSaraydarianUniversity.org</u> or write to us.

Ordering Information

All of Torkom's creative works and TSG's products are available for purchase at www.tsgfoundation.org

lisher for additional information regarding:

— Complete list of lecture tapes and videos
($2 postage for each list - available for free on the website)

— Placement on mailing list for continuous updates

— A free copy of our newsletter *Outreach* (latest edition, plus archived copies available on the website)

— **Join our Book Club at no charge. (Receive a 20% discount with each new release by Torkom Saraydarian. Each new book is mailed to you automatically as soon as it is released.) Send us a written approval to include you in the Book Club.**

Additional copies of *Angels and Devas*

U.S. $6.00

Contact us for shipping and handling rates. For international orders please indicate whether you want surface or air.

T.S.G. Publishing Foundation, Inc.
P.O. Box 7068
Cave Creek, AZ 85327–7068
United States of America
TEL: (480) 502–1909
FAX: (480) 502–0713
E-Mail:info@tsgfoundation.org
For additional information about the publisher, visit the website at: www.tsgfoundation.org

P 34 – Joy food of angels